On the Board

200 Fast, Fun & Easy Warmer, Filler and Fast-Finisher Activities

Other Books by Alphabet Publishing

50 Activities for the First Day of School
by Walton Burns

"A treasure trove of creative and practical icebreakers, warm-ups, and activities for building a cohesive class."
– Dorothy Zemach

50 Activities for the First Day of School features:
- Classic icebreakers and name games
- Fun ways to start teaching on the first day
- New innovative activities to build rapport
- Practical ideas to set the rules from day one
- Engaging ways to introduce the course right away
- Effective methods of assessing your students' language level

Free Teacher Resources and Discounts

If you like this book, sign up for our mailing list on our website, www.alphabetpublishingbooks.com.

Get our newsletter of great resources, including activities we love, articles we're thinking about, a dose of teacher inspiration, and of course deals and giveaways that won't be announced anywhere else.

And visit our site to read our blog, find free resources, and get in touch so we can improve our products

On the Board

200 Fast, Fun & Easy Warmer, Filler and Fast-Finisher Activities
By Walton Burns

ISBN: 978-0-9977628-3-9 (print)
ISBN: 978-0-9977628-2-2 (e-book)

Published by
Alphabet Publishing
1204 Main Street #172
Branford, Connecticut 06405 USA
(203) 442-5222

info@alphabetpublishingbooks.com
www.alphabetpublishingbooks.com

On the Board

200 Fast, Fun & Easy Warmer, Filler and Fast-Finisher Activities

Walton Burns

We are a small, independent publishing company that specializes in resources for teachers in the area of English language learning. We believe that a good teacher is resourceful, with a well-stocked toolkit full of ways to elicit, explain, guide, review, encourage and inspire. We help stock that teacher toolkit by providing teachers with books of practical and useful activities and techniques

Contents

Introduction

In 2005, I began volunteering at an English language center in Astana, Kazakhstan. Every Monday night, anywhere from 10 to 40 people would come to practice speaking English. Most of the participants were high school or university students planning to study in an English-speaking university. But there were also adults who needed English for work, retirees who wanted to keep up their English for fun, and other English teachers or trainers. It was a fun, low-pressure group and you never knew who would show up from week to week. So I'd just pick a theme, prepare a few questions and off we'd go.

I also developed a habit of opening class by putting a proverb or saying related to the day's theme on the board. I'd then asked students: What do you think this proverb means? Do you agree with it or disagree with it? Do you know a similar proverb in Russian or Kazakh?

They loved it.

From there, I moved on to include puzzles, riddles, jokes, even funny headlines. Soon I was writing down anything I could find or anything I came up with that could work as one of these quick warm-ups or do-nows.

In short, this collection became one of my go-to teaching tools. I'm hoping it will fast become one of yours, as well.

On the Board

These activities are no prep, and easy to use. Students can do them on their own, so they stay busy while you're setting up the lesson or checking attendance. And once students get into the habit of looking for it, you can throw something up on the board and let them have at it for the first 3-5 minutes of class.

The book is divided into different kinds of activities: Brainteasers & Riddles, Jokes, Headlines, Proverbs and Quotations. Before each section, I've given some suggestions on how to use that kind of activity in class and ways to extend them beyond the first 5 minutes of class. I've also added lots of space in the margin to leave comments and notes. Add your own favorite jokes or proverbs or note down what vocabulary students struggled with.

In general, these make great warmers or do-nows, although they may be a bit shorter than the average do-now. You can also use them as fillers or compile a bunch of them into a "quiz" for students—it's a great thing to add to your Fast Finisher file!

Brainteasers & Riddles

Brainteasers and riddles, even silly jokes, are great critical thinking activities. They give students something to think about. I've selected puzzles here that have students grappling with language. Each riddle is followed by the answer in *italics*, and an explanation, if necessary. Obviously, write the riddle down by itself.

You should alert students to the nature of the answer. Is it a pun or a riddle or a serious logical puzzle? It can be quite frustrating to work with what you think is a serious puzzle only to discover that it's a joke.

How to use them

- Have students try to solve it.

- Once they solve it, have students write down the solution and what is tricky about it.

- Have students create a similar puzzle or joke or riddle.

- Ask students to translate a riddle. How well does it translate? Can they do it literally or do they have to adapt it?

On the Board

Riddles about Letters

These riddles center on letters or words. It's important to tell students that. Without knowing the answer is a letter, students will take these riddles seriously and find them quite difficult. The answer often relies on word-play such as the word "tea" sounding like "t".

One way to tip students off is to do one as a class, then reveal the answer. You can then give them another one to do on their own.

What is the center of gravity?
The letter V.

What starts with "P" and ends with "E" and has more than 1000 letters?
A post office!

How do you make the number one disappear?
Add the letter g and it's "gone"

What occurs once in every minute, twice in every moment, yet never in a thousand years?
The letter m.

We see it once in a year, twice in a week, and never in a day. What is it?
The letter e

What's the difference between here and there?
The letter t

What do an island and the letter T have in common?
They are both in the middle of water.

What is at the end of a rainbow?
The letter w.

What starts with t, ends with t, and is filled with t?
A teapot. (The last t refers to the word tea, which is pronounced the same as the letter)

What 5-letter word becomes shorter when you add two letters to it?
Short. The two letters you add are -er, turning short into shorter

There's a seven-letter word. Take two letters away and you have eight. What word is it?
weights or freight

I am the beginning of sorrow, and the end of sickness. You cannot express happiness without me. I am always in risk, yet never in danger. You may find me in the sun, but I am never seen out of darkness.
The letter s

How many letters are in the alphabet?
11 "The alphabet" is 11 letters long.

On the Board

What do you find in the middle of Toronto?
The letter o

What starts with an "e," ends with an "e" and
usually contains only one letter?
*An envelope. The one letter here refers to a
written letter.*

The first two letters of an English word refer to a
man, the first three refer to a woman, the first
four to a great man and the whole word to a
great woman.
Heroine: He-Her-Hero-Heroine

Codes

These are puzzles that depend on guessing what letters stand for in a kind of code. The answer takes the form of a well-known fact and the letters are always the first letter of the word they stand for.

I've provided the code and then the answer in *italics* afterwards. Obviously, put only the code up.

How to use them

These tend to work best if you use more than one at a time. Put a few related ones up (all the ones about time, for example) and ask students, "What do the letters stand for?" As they catch on, these can go very fast, but it may take students a while at first.

These are fairly easy to think up so as a follow-up, you could have the students make their own questions and quiz each other.

60 S in a M
60 seconds in a minute

60 M in an H
60 minutes in an hour

On the Board

24 H in a D
24 hours in a day

7 D in a W
7 days in a week

4 W in a M
4 weeks in a month

30 or 31 D in a M
30 or 31 days in a month

12 M in a Y
12 months in a year

4 S in a Y
4 seasons in a year

100 Y in a C
100 years in a century

1000 Y in a M
1000 years in a millennium

4 W on a C
4 wheels on a car

4 L on a T
4 legs on a table

5 O in the W
5 oceans in the world

7 C in the W
7 continents in the world

3 S to a T
3 sides to a triangle

4 S to a S
4 sides to a square

5 S to a P
5 sides to a pentagon

6 S to a H
6 sides to a hexagon

8 S to an O
8 sides to an octagon

8 or 9 P in the SS
8 or 9 planets in the solar system
(depending on what you make of Pluto)

9 M of P
9 months of pregnancy

115 C E
115 chemical elements

52 W K on a P
52 white keys on a piano

On the Board

52 C in a D
52 cards in a deck

12 D of C
12 days of Christmas

90 D in a RT
90 degrees in a right triangle

11 P on a F or S T
11 players on football or soccer team

What's the next (and last) letter in this sequence?
J-F-M-A-M-J-J-A-S-O-N
D for December. These are the first letters of the months of the year

What's the next (and last) letter in this sequence?
M-T-W-T-F-S-
S for Sunday. These are the first letters of the days of the week.

Logic Puzzles

A logic puzzle requires students to think carefully before answering. They will often need to refer to their pre-existing knowledge. Of course, some of the more fun logic puzzles try to trick you into guessing the wrong answer. So make sure your students read carefully and think through their assumptions.

What do the numbers 11, 69, and 88 all have in common?
They read the same right side up and upside down.

Christmas Day is one week before New Year's Day, the first day of the New Year. They always fall on the same day of the week. But in what year did they both happen in the same year?
Every year there's a New Year's Day and a Christmas Day!

If you were running a race and you passed the person in second place, what place would you be in?
second place.

On the Board

The capital of Turkey is a long word. Can you spell it?
i-t. The question literally asks you to spell the word "it".

If a rooster is standing in the middle of a slanted barn roof, which side would its egg roll down?
Neither. Roosters don't lay eggs.

A man went outside on a rainy day. He didn't have an umbrella or a hat. His clothes got soaked, yet not a single hair on his head got wet. How did it happen?
The man was bald.

A cowboy rides into town on Friday, stays for four days, and leaves on Friday. How is it possible?
His horse's name was Friday.

What two things can you never eat for breakfast?
Lunch and Dinner (or supper).

Which weighs more, a pound of feathers or a pound of bricks?
Both weigh a pound.

Some months have 31 days but how many months have 28 days?
All of them have at least 28 days!

What can you catch, but not throw?
A cold

There are 3 apples. You take 2. How many do you have?
You have 2. It says clearly, "You take 2."

How far can you walk into a forest?
Halfway. After that you are walking out of the forest.

Beth's mother has three daughters. One is named Laura and the other one is Sara. What is the name of the third daughter?
Beth. The question says Beth's mother

A plane crashes right on the border between the US and Canada. 15 people die. Where do they bury the survivors?
Nowhere. Survivor means the people who lived.

Why is it illegal in the US to marry your widow's sister?
If you have a widow, it means you are dead.

There is a red one-story house and everything in it is red. The tables are red, the chairs are red, and the piano is red. What color is the staircase?
It's a one-story house. There is no staircase.

A man builds a rectangular house in such a way that all sides face south. A bear walks by. What color is the bear?
White. He built the house at the North Pole, the only place where all directions are south.

On the Board

A man was driving his truck. His lights were not on. The moon was not out. Up ahead, a woman was crossing the street. How did he see her?
It's day time. That's why the moon wasn't out and his lights weren't on.

A man leaves home and turns left three times, only to return home facing two men wearing masks. Who are those two men?
A catcher and an umpire. He is playing baseball.

A man has a heavy barrel full of water. He puts something in the barrel that makes it much lighter. What does he put in it?
A hole

The next four riddles go together: How do you put an elephant in the refrigerator?
Open the refrigerator and put the elephant in.

How do you put a giraffe in a refrigerator?
Open the door, take the elephant out, and put the giraffe in.

The Lion King holds a meeting and invites all the animals. All of them come but one. Which animal doesn't come?
The lion. He was already there because he invited everyone.

You are also going to the Lion King's meeting but you have to cross a river inhabited by crocodiles.

How do you get across without being eaten by the crocodiles?

Just walk across. The crocodiles are at the meeting

On the Board

"What Am I?" Riddles

This genre of classic riddles asks the students to guess what is being described. They are challenging, because the riddles are often phrased to confuse. Students have to think carefully.

The dirtier I get, the whiter I get. What am I?
A chalkboard

No matter how big or small I am, you cannot fill me up with all the water in the ocean. What am I?
A sieve.

The more of me you take, the more of me you leave behind you.
Footsteps.

What has 88 keys but can't open a single door?
A piano

What has a neck but no head?
A bottle

What goes around and around the wood, but never into the woods?
The bark of a tree.

What is served, but never eaten?
A tennis ball.

What goes through towns and over hills but never moves?
A road

They come out at night without being called, and are lost in the day without being stolen. What are they?
Stars

What can you hear but not touch or see?
Your voice.

What runs around a house, but never moves?
A fence.

What flies without wings?
Time

What comes down but never goes up?
Rain

What goes up but never comes down?
Your age

What has a head but never weeps, has a bed but never sleeps, can run but never walks, and has a bank but no money?
A river

The more I eat, the bigger I get but if I drink, I die. What am I?
A fire.

On the Board

What is put on a table and cut, but never eaten?
A deck of cards

What's full of holes but still holds water?
A sponge.

What word in the dictionary is spelled incorrectly?
Incorrectly.

What is always coming but never arrives?
Tomorrow

What can travel around the world while staying in a corner?
A stamp.

What gets wetter and wetter the more it dries?
A towel

What has hands but can't hold anything?
A clock.

If you have it, you want to share it. If you share it, you don't have it. What is it?
A secret

What is light as a feather but no one can hold it for more than a minute?
Your breath.

What can run even though it doesn't have legs?
A drop of water.

If you say its name, you break it.
Silence

What goes upstairs and downstairs but never moves?
A staircase.

What never asks questions but is often answered?
A doorbell.

What belongs to you but other people use it more than you?
Your name.

I have a large piggy bank in the shape of a cube. It's 1 foot wide, 1 foot tall and 1 foot high. How many quarters can I place in my empty piggy bank?
Just one. Then it won't be empty.

A boy at the beach makes 3 piles of sand. A girl makes 4 piles of sand. If they put them together, how many piles of sand will they have?
Just one big pile of sand.

What has to be broken before you can use it?
An egg

Puns and Jokes

Puns are a kind of joke that uses word play. Puns use words that sound similar, or a word that has more than one meaning. Students need to understand that the answers to these questions require thinking about word sounds, and that the answer is silly, not entirely logical.

What kind of nut has no shell?
A doughnut.

What kind of coat can be put on only when its wet?
A coat of paint.

Why is it easy to weigh fish?
They have their own scales.

What room can't be entered?
A mushroom.

What kind of tree can you carry in your hand?
A palm tree.

Why is six afraid of seven?
Because seven eight (ate) nine.

What lets you look throw walls?
A window!

What two keys can't open doors?
A monkey and a donkey.

Where do fish keep their money?
A riverbank.

What is gray, and has a tail and a trunk?
A mouse on vacation!

What question can a person ask all day long and get a different answer to every time, even though all the answers are correct.
What time is it?

What do you call a boomerang that doesn't work?
A stick

How does the ocean say hello to the beach?
It waves.

What did one math book say to the other math book?
I have a lot of problems.

What do you call a dog with a clock around its neck?
A watch dog.

What do you get when you cross a frog and a hare?
A bunny ribbit

Funny Headlines

When I was young, I had a book of puzzles and games that included a section on funny headlines. I've always loved them and my students do too. It's a great way to get them analyzing grammar and thinking about double meanings.

As you will quickly note, some of these are a bit risqué so keep the ages of your learners in mind. Others are outdated which may or may not be a problem depending on your students.

How to use them

- Ask students to find the mistake or the funny part. Often the joke comes from a *double entendre*, where a word has two meanings which leads to two possible interpretations of a sentence.

- Ask students to rewrite or correct the headline so that the meaning is clear.

- Ask students to write a short summary of the newspaper article, either the serious real news story or the unintentionally funny one.

- As follow-up, students can examine a newspaper looking for headlines that might be misinterpreted. You can also have students make a list of words with two meanings and then try to make their own *double entendre*.

Grandmother of Eight Makes Hole in One

Deaf Mute Gets New Hearing in Killing

Police Begin Campaign to Run Down Jaywalkers

House Passes Gas Tax onto Senate

Two Convicts Avoid the Noose, Jury Hung

Cemetery Residents Making a Comeback

Milk Drinkers Are Turning to Powder

Safety Experts Say School Bus Passengers Should Be Belted

Quarter of a Million Chinese Live on Water

Farmer Bill Dies in House

Iraqi Head Seeks Arms

Queen Mary Having Bottom Scraped

Prostitutes Appeal to Pope

Panda Mating Fails — Veterinarian Takes Over

NJ Judge to Rule on Nude Beach

On the Board

Child's Stool Great for Use in Garden

Dr. Ruth to Talk About Sex with Newspaper Editors

Soviet Virgin Lands Short of Goal Again

Organ Festival Ends in Smashing Climax

Eye Drops off Shelf

Squad Helps Dog Bite Victim

Dealers Will Hear Car Talk at Noon

Enraged Cow Injures Farmer with Ax

Lawmen from Mexico Barbecue Guests

Miners Refuse to Work After Death

Two Soviet Ships Collide — One Dies

Two Sisters Reunite after Eighteen Years at Checkout Counter

Never Withhold Sickness from Loved One

Nicaragua Sets Goal to Wipe Out Literacy

Drunk Drivers Paid $1,000 in 1984

Autos Killing 110 a Day, Let's Resolve to Do Better

Smokers Are Productive, But Death Cuts Efficiency

Cold Wave Linked to Temperatures

Child's Death Ruins Couple's Holiday

Blind Woman Gets New Kidney from Dad She Hasn't Seen in Years

Man Is Fatally Slain

Something Went Wrong in Jet Crash, Experts Say

Death Causes Loneliness, Feeling of Isolation

Students Cook and Serve Grandparents

Mayor Tells Homeless Protestors to Go Home

City Council Runs Out of Time to Discuss Shorter Meetings

One Armed Man Applauds the Kindness of Strangers

Police Kill Man with Stolen TV

Police Raid Gun Store, Find Weapons

Missing Baby Found in Sandwich

New Sick Policy Requires 2-Day Notice

Homeless Survive Winter: Now What?

Proverbs

Proverbs are a fun way to have students think about language and idioms. Some students enjoy memorizing proverbs and using them in conversation, so you may find that students love these do-nows. There's also a lot of follow-up you can do with proverbs, such as introducing the theme of the class or having students write an exegesis or summary.

I've tried to curate proverbs that aren't too idiomatic or too difficult to figure out. However, you may need to simplify or rewrite some of these, or step in to explain some of the idioms.

How to Use them

- Ask students to figure out what the proverb means.

- Ask students to decide, or discuss in pairs, whether they agree or disagree with the proverb.

- Ask students to think of a saying or proverb from their culture that has a similar meaning.

- Ask students to try to translate the proverb to their own language. Does it make sense or do they need to change the words?

- Ask them to think of an example from literature, history, or their own lives that the proverb applies to.

When in Rome, do as the Romans do.

Don't bite off more than you can chew.

Actions speak louder than words.

If you can't stand the heat, get out of the kitchen.

A leopard cannot change its spots.

Lightning never strikes twice in the same place.

Misery loves company.

No news is good news.

Rome wasn't built in a day.

Two's company, but three's a crowd.

Where there's smoke, there's fire.

The way to a man's heart is through his stomach.

You can't have your cake and eat it too.

On the Board

You reap what you sow.

Bad news travels fast.

His bark is worse than his bite

Better safe than sorry.

The best things in life are free.

Curiosity killed the cat

An apple a day keeps the doctor away.

Better late than never.

Don't put all your eggs in one basket.

Haste makes waste.

There's more than one way to skin a cat.

There's no such thing as a free lunch.

Don't cry over spilled milk.

Don't judge a book by its cover.

If it isn't broken, don't fix it.

Don't throw the baby out with the bathwater.

A watched pot never boils.

Don't put the cart before the horse.

Beggars can't be choosers.

Every cloud has a silver lining.

You can't make an omelet without breaking a few eggs.

A picture is worth a thousand words.

Actions speak louder than words.

People who live in glass houses should not throw stones.

You can choose your friends, but you can't choose your family

Clothes make the man.

When the going gets tough, the tough get going.

No man is an island.

The grass is always greener on the other side of the fence.

Love is blind.

Never look a gift horse in the mouth.

Birds of a feather flock together.

On the Board

The early bird catches the worm.

Two heads are better than one.

A chain is only as strong as its weakest link.

You can lead a horse to water, but you can't make him drink.

The early bird catches the worm.

A penny saved is a penny earned.

Absence makes the heart grow fonder.

The pen is mightier than the sword.

The squeaky wheel gets the grease.

A bird in the hand is worth two in the bush

Any port in a storm.

Don't bite the hand that feeds you.

A fool and his money are soon parted.

Necessity is the mother of invention.

There's no place like home.

All that glitters is not gold.

All that is gold does not glitter.

If you can't beat 'em, join 'em.

One man's trash is another man's treasure.

One bad apple spoils the bunch.

Look before you leap.

You can't take it with you when you go.

Practice what you preach.

All good things much come to an end.

Experience is the best teacher.

Sometimes less is more.

Do unto others as you would like to have them do unto you.

Judge a person by the company they keep.

Too many cooks spoil the soup.

You can't teach an old dog new tricks.

A rolling stone gathers no moss.

As you make your bed, so must you lie in it.

Quotations

Quotations are much like proverbs, and in fact many proverbs are quotations whose origin we have forgotten.

Like proverbs, quotations expose students to idioms and some non-standard grammar. I have simplified some of the quotations, and you may feel the need to simplify them further.

You may want to follow these up with a discussion of the person who said the quote and the context of the quote. What work or speech did it come from? Of course, students can also do this research work for homework.

How to use them

- Ask students to figure out what the quotation means.

- Ask students to decide, or discuss in pairs, whether they agree or disagree with the quotation.

- Ask students to think of a quotation or perhaps a proverb from their culture that has a similar meaning.

- Ask them to think of an example from literature, history, or their own lives that the quotation applies to.

- Have students research the person who said the quote and report back on who they were and what the quote might have meant in their context.

Life is 10% what happens to you and 90% how you react to it.
- Charles R. Swindoll

Is it possible to have too much of a good thing?
- Shakespeare (adapted)

It is people who make a city, not walls or ships
- Thucydides

Do what you can with what you have, where you are.
- Theodore Roosevelt

There is only one thing in the world worse than being talked about, and that is not being talked about.
- Oscar Wilde

What we think, we become.
- Buddha

On the Board

A problem is a chance for you to do your best.
- Duke Ellington

Always forgive your enemies — nothing annoys
them so much.
- Oscar Wilde

But love is blind, and lovers cannot see.
- Shakespeare

If you only read the books that everyone else is
reading, you can only think what everyone else is
thinking.
- Haruki Murakami

It is easier to forgive an enemy than to forgive a
friend.
- William Blake

Experience is simply the name we give our
mistakes.
- Oscar Wilde

Music is the food of love.
- Shakespeare (adapted)

Don't grieve. Anything you lose comes round in
another form.
- Rumi

Anyone who has never made a mistake, has never
tried anything new.
- Albert Einstein

The only thing I fear more than change is no change. The business of being static makes me nuts.
- Twyla Tharp

Don't sweat the small stuff, and it's all small stuff.
- Dr. Richard Carlson

Keep your friends close, but your enemies closer.
- Machiavelli

What's in a name? That which we call a rose by any other name would smell as sweet.
- Shakespeare (adapted)

If you don't know where you are going, any road will get you there.
- Lewis Carroll

It takes two to speak truth—one to speak and another to hear.
- Henry David Thoreau

The only thing we have to fear is...fear itself.
- Franklin Delano Roosevelt

Be true to yourself and you cannot lie to anyone.
- Shakespeare (adapted)

When you do things from your soul, you feel a river moving in you, a joy.
- Rumi

On the Board

The greatest barrier to success is the fear of failure.
- Sven Goran Eriksson

As I grow older, I pay less attention to what men say. I just watch what they do.
- Andrew Carnegie

There is nothing either good or bad, but thinking makes it so.
- Shakespeare

Man is least himself when he talks in his own person. Give him a mask, and he will tell you the truth.
- Oscar Wilde

It isn't over till it's over.
- Yogi Berra

Age is an issue of mind over matter. If you don't mind, it doesn't matter.
- Mark Twain

I am free of all prejudices. I hate everyone equally.
- WC Fields

To live is the rarest thing in the world. Most people exist, that is all.
- Oscar Wilde

We are all in the gutter, but some of us are looking at the stars.
- Oscar Wilde

Only a mediocre person is always at his best.
- W. Somerset Maugham

Our lives teach us who we are.
- Salman Rushdie

You cannot find peace by avoiding life.
- Virginia Woolf

Against the assault of laughter, nothing can stand.
- Mark Twain

What is a cynic? A man who knows the price of everything and the value of nothing.
- Oscar Wilde

Be not afraid of greatness: some are born great, some achieve greatness, and some have greatness thrust upon them.
- Shakespeare

Our lives begin the day we become silent about things that matter.
- Dr. Martin Luther King

It's fine to celebrate success but it is more important to heed the lessons of failure.
- Bill Gates

All great deeds and all great thoughts have a ridiculous beginning.
- Albert Camus

On the Board

All the world's a stage, and all the men and women merely players. They have their exits and their entrances; And one man in his time plays many parts.
 - Shakespeare (adapted)

Faith is taking the first step even when you don't see the whole staircase.
- Martin Luther King, Jr.

Imagination is more important than knowledge. Knowledge is limited. Imagination encircles the world.
- Albert Einstein

The glamour of being forbidden must not be underestimated.
- Salman Rushdie

The pen is mightier than the sword.
 - Edward Bulwer-Lytton

Live as if you were to die tomorrow. Learn as if you were to live forever.
- Mahatma Gandhi

 Disbelief in magic can force a poor soul into believing in government and business.
- Tom Robbins

There are two kinds of people in technology: those who understand what they do not manage, and those who manage what they do not

understand.
- Putt's Law

Never despair; but if you do, work on in despair.
- Edmund Burke

It is the mark of an educated mind to be able to entertain a thought without accepting it.
- Aristotle

You can fool all the people some of the time, and some of the people all the time, but you cannot fool all the people all the time.
- Abraham Lincoln

Women who seek to be equal with men lack ambition.
- Timothy Leary

Management is doing things right; leadership is doing the right things.
- Peter Drucker

It is better to travel well than to arrive.
- Buddha

It's so much easier to suggest solutions when you don't know too much about the problem.
- Malcolm Forbes

All grown-ups were once children... but only few of them remember it.
- Antoine de Saint-Exupéry

On the Board

The point of living and of being an optimist, is to be foolish enough to believe the best is yet to come.
- Peter Ustinov

A little learning is a dangerous thing; Drink deep, or taste not the Pierian spring.
- Alexander Pope

War is a cowardly escape from the problems of peace.
- Thomas Mann

No one can make you feel inferior without your consent.
- Eleanor Roosevelt

An ignorant person is one who doesn't know what you have just found out.
- Will Rogers

Power tends to corrupt and absolute power tends to corrupt absolutely.
- Lord Acton

Free advice is worth the price.
- Robert Half

I have never met a man so ignorant that I couldn't learn something from him.
- Galileo Galilei

The average person thinks he isn't.
- Father Larry Lorenzoni

Good teaching is one-fourth preparation and three-fourths theater.
- Gail Godwin

Failure is not the only punishment for laziness; there is also the success of others.
- Jules Renard (1864 - 1910)

Lost time is never found again.
- Ben Franklin

Men are never so likely to settle a question rightly as when they discuss it freely.
- Lord Macaulay

I am not afraid of an army of lions led by a sheep; I am afraid of an army of sheep led by a lion.
- Alexander the Great

History repeats itself, first as tragedy, second as farce.
-Karl Marx

Even if you are a minority of one, the truth is the truth.
- Mahatma Gandhi

If something can go wrong, it will.
- Murphy's Law

More Activity Ideas

These are nine other activities I often use as do-nows. These activity types are highly adaptable so that you can introduce a topic or review previous material.

Key Concept

Ask each student to think about the last lesson and write one important or key concept on the board. This creates a list of things students think were important from the past lesson. You can then discuss the list, ask students to come up with follow-up questions, or have them copy the concepts down as a sort of study guide.

As a variation, you could have students write a lingering question they have from the past lesson. Then other students can try to answer each other's questions.

Multiple Choice Trivia

They have trivia questions on boards outside stores to draw customers in. You can put one on the board to draw students in. If you can match the question to your lesson, so much the better.

Think of a fun and interesting fact that it is related to your topic, something like:

> Which country is the biggest in the world?
> A) The US B) Canada C) Russia.

Or you can give students an actual problem to solve related to the lesson. As an ESL / EFL teacher, I might write something like:

> Choose the right answer to go in the blank.
> Give the dog ___ bone back.
> A) its B) it C) it's

Have students give their answer. It can be fun to take a poll, or have students discuss why they think they are right before revealing the answer.

Review Quiz

A short quiz can act as a kind of warmer. Put 1-3 questions on the board that review key concepts from the homework or the lesson before. Even a simple vocabulary test such as "Write down the definitions of the words on the board" works as a nice review.

Word Association

Put a key word on the board. If your theme is family, you could write "Family" or "Love" or "Home". Have each student say or write down the first four things that come to their mind when they think of the key word. Students can then share as a class or in small pairs. You can also write their answers on the board to build vocabulary or use for discussion later.

Spell it Out

Put a key word on the board and have students see how many words they can spell using the letters from that word. This works best with longer words and phrases such as "Christmas", or "Halloween", or "The Olympic Games".

Guess the Theme

Write words associated with the theme on the board and have students guess what the theme is. If your theme is a category such as "Food", you could write different kinds of food and ask students what all those words have in common. Note that to have this one last more than a minute or two, you might have to be a bit cryptic.

Guess the Keywords

Write the theme of the class on the board. Then ask students to write all the words they expect to read or see about this topic. When class gets started, you can also have them put a line through the words on the board when they do encounter them—in a reading, say. Then you can close class by talking about their expectations versus what they actually read or talked about.

Short Reading Comprehension

A short reading such as a paragraph or a brief news article can also work as a warm-up. Follow it up with questions that connect the reading to the theme of the class. It can even be extended into a proper Do-Now or Bell ringer if you write those questions down.

Discussion Question

Write a provocative question that you want students to discuss in class, or plan to provide an answer to during class. Students sit, write down their answer and then brainstorm as many reasons as they can for their answer.

This can be the precursor to a class discussion, debate, or even the beginning of pre-writing an essay.

About the Author

Walton Burns is a teacher and award-winning materials writer from Connecticut. He began his career in 2001, teaching in the Peace Corps in Vanuatu, an island chain in the South Pacific. Since then, he has taught in Central Asia and his native country. His students have been a diverse group, including Russian oil executives, Afghan high school students, and Chinese video game champions.

As a writer, he has been on the author team of two textbooks and written lesson plans and activities for private language schools. He is currently chair of the Materials Writing Interest Section of the TESOL Association, the international association for English language professionals.

He is also the author of *50 Activities for the First Day of School* by Alphabet Publishing and a new book of mystery activities from Pro-Lingua Associates, *31 Mysteries to Solve Clue by Clue*.

Check out his portfolio at www.waltonburns.com and his occasionally updated blog at www.englishadvantageblog.com.

Thank you

If you enjoyed this book, and you tried these activities in your classroom, won't you please take a moment to drop us a line at info@alphabetpublishingbooks.com? We'd love to know how you used these in the classroom, and how it went.

If we include your idea on our blog or mailing list, we'll reward you with a coupon code good for use on our site

CPSIA information can be obtained
at www.ICGtesting.com
Printed in the USA
BVHW041147020421
604042BV00014B/356